# BipQuiz

## 100 QUESTIONS & ANSWERS

# Nature

# BipQuiz

## 100 QUESTIONS & ANSWERS

# Nature

*Illustrations by Florence MacKenzie*

**Sterling Publishing Co., Inc.  New York**

10   9   8   7   6   5   4   3   2   1
Published by Sterling Publishing Company, Inc.
387 Park Avenue South, New York, N.Y. 10016
© 1994 by InfoMedia Communication
English translation © 1994 by Sterling Publishing Co., Inc.
Distributed in Canada by Sterling Publishing
% Canadian Manda Group, P.O. Box 920, Station U
Toronto, Ontario, Canada M8Z 5P9
*Printed in France - Publiphotoffset, 93500 Pantin*
Sterling ISBN 0-8069-0939-0

# How to Use the BipPen

The BipPen must be held straight to point to the black dot.

Point to a black dot.

●

A continuous sound (beeeep) and a red light mean that you've chosen the wrong answer.

Point to a black dot.

●

A discontinuous sound (beep beep beep) and a green light mean that you've chosen the right answer.

Keep your BipPen for our other books.

# Headings

Each question belongs to a specific heading.
Each heading is identified by a color.

## Edible and useful plants

## Trees and flowers

## Feeding and reproduction

## Landscape and farming

## Various

**1**

T he scientific name for plants is composed of 2 Latin names. The first is capitalized and denotes the genus, and the second, which is not capitalized, denotes the species. These names are used by:

botanists ●
engineers ■
electricians ▲

**2**

T he first plants lived in water. Millions of years later, some species have adapted to life on dry land. Plants that live in water are called:

amphibious ●
swimming ■
aquatic ▲

There are a hundred or so species of oak throughout the world. Its solid wood is often used in construction (furniture, carpentry . . .). Its fruit is known as:

ilex
acorn
rose

4

Plants make part of their food thanks to a process called photosynthesis. They make sugars by using solar energy by using their:

chlorophyll
sap
resin

T here are two types of tree: leafy ones, with long and flat leaves, and conifers, whose fruit is often called a:

conif
apple
cone

S ome carnivorous plants attract their prey by diffusing the smell of their prey's food. However, like all green plants, they engage in:

photosynthesis
photogeny
photographic synthesis

The world's largest flower is the *Rafflesia arnoldii*. This parasitic plant, found on the island of Sumatra, can measure over 36" (90 cm) in diameter. It can weigh:

4½ lbs. (2 kgs) ●
11 lbs. (5 kgs) ■
over 15 lbs. ▲
  (7 kgs)

Lianas are climbing plants with inter-twining, flexible stems. What famous character travelled through the jungle from liana to liana?

Bullwinkle ●
Tarzan ■
Goofy ▲

$A$quatic plants, which are often only partially submerged, develop mostly in ponds, lakes, and rivers. The Egyptians used one to write on:

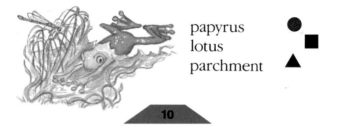

papyrus ●

lotus ■

parchment ▲

$T$o survive droughts, desert plants store water in their very long roots. So as to avoid any loss of water, some have replaced their leaves with thorns. This is true of:

fig trees ●

thistles ■

cacti ▲

P lants are often used for pharmaceutical and cosmetic purposes. They have curative or beautifying properties when taken in small doses. One of the plants most commonly used for such purposes is the:

dandelion
jojoba
crocus

F or most plants to reproduce, the seeds of the stamen (male part) must fertilize the pistil's (female part) ovules. These seeds are called:

corolla
petal
pollen

Pollen is transported to the flower's female organs by insects or by the wind. Insects are covered with pollen when they land on a flower to:

mutiny    ●
tickle    ■
gather    ▲
nectar

Flowers are colorful and perfumed so as to attract insects. In return for pollination, insects feed on the flowers':

nectar    ●
honey    ■
ambrosia    ▲

B otanists specialize in the study of plants. They brought a large number of our plants from countries that were explored beginning in the 19th century. Fuchsias come from South America, while tulips come from:

Asia
Africa
New Zealand

16

T he place where young trees are grown before being planted in gardens or forests is called:

a shed
a tree nursery
a den

S ome imported plants, like orchids, are used to a tropical climate. Horticulturists create special areas for them, known as:

greenhouses ●
shambles ■
jars ▲

T he olive tree is quite common in Mediterranean regions and keeps its leaves during the winter. The green fruits turn black when they mature. What is extracted from olives?

powder ●
poison ■
oil ▲

The melting of snow feeds mountain streams. These cold waters change into rivers that ultimately flow into:

big rivers
lakes
the sea

Rice is planted in flooded rice fields. It is picked 3 to 6 months later after draining the field. The moment at which plants or fruits of any kind are collected is generally called the:

harvest
sowing
donation

L eafy trees have simple (each with its own stem) or complex (each leaf is divided into leaflets attached to the same stem) leaves. Coniferous leaves are shaped like:

propellers ●

needles ■

lobes ▲

B ees make honey from the nectar they collect from flowers. The beekeeper then collects the honey, with which one makes:

caramel ●

fruitcake ■

nougat ▲

We currently use only 200 of the 80,000 known edible plants. Mostly, we eat members of the Graninae family, to which belong cereals and:

mushrooms
lichen
sugarcane

It is possible to dye fabrics by boiling them with some flowers. Chamomile gives orange, broom gives green, and the water lily gives:

black
yellow
pink

A tree is a large plant with a trunk and wooden branches. Unlike trees and bushes, shrubs have no:

leaves    ●

trunk    ■

branches    ▲

During the autumn, most leaves change color and fall from the trees. During the summer, forests are humid and cool, for the hotter the weather gets, the more trees:

die    ●

lose their sap    ■

sweat    ▲

A pples are ready for harvest in autumn. They are kept in a cold and dark place throughout the winter and used to make which beverage?

cider ●
beer ■
champagne ▲

C ambium is a cell tissue that is specific to trees and lets them make new wood throughout their life. The number of rings found inside a trunk indicates:

the tree's age ●
the species ■
the branches ▲

The sugars formed by photosynthesis, and the water and mineral salts pumped up by the roots, form plants' nutritive substances, known as:

acids ●

vitamins ■

sap ▲

The birch is a tree that can grow in poor soil where no other tree can grow. It can live up to 80 or 100 years, and its wood is used to make:

shingles ●

matches ■

tools ▲

The truffle oak owes its name to the truffles that grow among its roots. Truffles are very expensive, because they're hard to find. Dogs and what other animals are specially trained to find them?

hens
foxes
pigs

The sequoia is native to the American west, and is the world's tallest tree. One of them reached 370 ft. (112 m), the equivalent of a building that has how many stories?

5
15
35

C acti are native to America. Their thorns protect them from the cold, heat, and animals. The saguaro is the largest cactus in the world. It can live 250 years and weigh:

1100 lbs. (500 kgs) ●
6 tons ■
100 tons ▲

**34**

A ll seashores are not alike. There are sand or pebble beaches, dunes, or high, steep rocks known as:

cliffs ●
mountains ■
tumuli ▲

S pruce can grow anywhere, although it prefers mountainous zones. It is used to make:

wooden clogs
Christmas trees
barbecue matches

C ereals are plants whose ears are full of seeds. One seed gives birth to tens more. Which of these plants is not a cereal?

sunflower
corn
rye

At low tide many shells can be seen stuck to the rocks. Some of these are winkles, limpets, and mussels. All of these animals are:

marsupials ●

mollusks ■

snails ▲

We do not always eat the same part of vegetables. We eat the cabbage's leaves, the bean's pod, the carrot's root, and the tomato's:

flower ●

fruit ■

bulb ▲

C hocolate is made from dry cocoa pods. These pods are then ground and mixed with sugar. Cocoa trees are prevalent in South America and:

Africa    
Australia
North America

T he linden tree's leaves are heart-shaped, and its fruit is grouped in bunches of 5 or 6. The flowers are picked and dried in June and used to make:

lipstick    
spices
(herbal) tea

Plant and tree diseases are usually caused by parasites that suck on plant sap. Young shoots are often the victims of aphids, whose greatest enemy is:

the ladybug ●
the snail ■
the earthworm ▲

The record for slowest plant growth is held by the plants from the Arctic's coldest regions (the Sitka pine grows 12″ (30 cm) in a century). The record for quickest growth—3½ ft. (1 m) a day—is held by:

ivy ●
bamboo ■
bramble ▲

Tea, like coffee, contains a stimulant. Tea comes from the tea bush, which is grown in hot climates. The country that produces the most tea is:

Japan
England
India

The fruit is that part of the tree that contains the seed. The fruit isn't always edible for man. Which of these trees doesn't have an edible fruit?

walnut
fir
chestnut

During the autumn, plants start to metabolize more slowly. Tree sap travels down to the roots, and most trees lose their leaves in order to protect themselves against the cold. These leaves are called:

deciduous ●

falling ■

bald ▲

Lichens can put up with very cold temperatures by producing an acid that interrupts their vital functions and protects them from extremes of weather. Lichens form the main food source in the tundra for:

reindeer ●

fox ■

camel ▲

Water is essential to life on earth. It is mostly in liquid form, but it changes to ice at 32°F (0°C). Above 212°F (100°C) it becomes:

cotton    ●

snow    ■

steam    ▲

Ferns are generally found in forests. Their leaves are curled in upon themselves, and they unfurl in spring. It was long thought that ferns could render people:

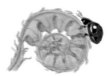

insane    ●

intelligent    ■

invisible    ▲

Wheat germinates by feeding on the nutrients in its own seed. Having become a green shoot, it uses its roots to gather nutrients. Once it has matured, it develops a cluster of seeds known as:

straw
the ear
the stem

A tree branch bears leaves and flowers. It can branch out, and buds grow on its tips. The tree that flowers earliest in the spring is:

oak
maple
magnolia

## 51

Mosses feed exclusively on air and rainfall, since they lack roots. They can nonetheless put up with drought for a few years. How many species are there?

between 500 and 2000 ●
between 5000 and 10,000 ■
over 20,000 ▲

## 52

Starting in autumn, tree leaves fall. Once on the ground, they protect the tree's roots. When they decompose, they integrate with the vegetable matter on the ground to form:

ficus ●
humus ■
mucus ▲

The natural colorant tannin is extracted from trees and is used to color leather. Wood is used to make furniture, musical instruments, and:

paper ●
gas ■
leather ▲

The longest roots ever found were those of a South African fig tree, 400 ft. (120 m). But if the measure of both roots and radicles is taken, the record is held by rye, which sometimes measures:

6.25 miles (10 km) ●
62.5 miles (100 km) ■
375 miles (600 km) ▲

A bonsai is a miniature tree that symbolizes the harmony between man and nature. It can live over 300 years and is passed from parent to child. It is part of the tradition of:

India ●

Japan ■

Tibet ▲

C onifers secrete a sticky and odorous substance from their trunks that's sometimes used in various medications. It is called:

resin ●

soap ■

chlorophyll ▲

R esearchers try to create new species. In order to facilitate transportation and stocking, they are attempting to create a tomato that's:

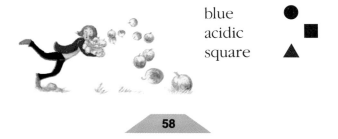

blue ●

acidic ■

square ▲

M istletoe is a parasite on trees, since it sucks their sap and kills them. It was sacred to the Gauls, whose druids cut down this parasite with:

a gold hatchet ●

a gold billhook ■

golden pruning shears ▲

T he cork oak's bark is used to make corks for bottles. Latex comes from the hevea tree and is transformed into:

rubber ●

cinnamon ■

wax ▲

S ugar comes from plants that are ground up. The juice is heated and then it crystallizes. These crystals must then be purified. Sugar comes from sugarcane and also from a type of:

carrot ●

beet ■

tomato ▲

F ruits are eaten when they're ripe and their flesh is sweet and tender. They are often rich in vitamins. Lemon is rich in vitamin C and was once very useful to seamen by preventing and curing:

yellow fever ●
scurvy ■
malaria ▲

A number of animals feed on plants. These animals are called:

vegetarians ●
vegetative ■
herbivores ▲

A certain mushroom ("stinkhorn") smells like rotting meat. To help ensure its reproduction, it thus attracts:

flies ●
worms ■
snails ▲

The air we breathe is a mix of many gases, nitrogen (78%) and oxygen (21%) in particular. Air is also composed of water vapor, carbon dioxide, and ozone. This mixture is called:

the atmosphere ●
the planisphere ■
space ▲

A nimals feed on plants or other animals. Most plants make their own food through photosynthesis. This, however, is not true of:

digitalis ●
oak ■
mushrooms ▲

P hytoplankton is composed of microscopic vegetable matter found in water. It is eaten by a group of microscopic animals, which are themsleves food for small fish and are called:

zoologist ●
zooplankton ■
microcosm ▲

Most mammals walk on 4 legs, except for man and some monkeys. Insects have 6 legs and spiders have:

10 legs ●
8 legs ■
12 legs ▲

Nature forces animals to adapt. The polar fox has small ears which waste little heat. On the other hand the desert fox has large ears to rid itself of heat and cool down. This fox is also called a:

jackal ●
fennec ■
dingo ▲

I n the countryside, farmers till the soil to grow the plants they eat. The most commonly cultivated plants are:

ferns ●

mosses ■

cereals ▲

T he place where a plant lives is called its habitat. In cold areas such as mountains, what have plants developed to combat the effects of wind?

short stems ●

large leaves ■

dark petals ▲

S ome trees suffer from pollution.
Combustible material (from power
plants and engines) emits gases which mix
with the water in the air and fall as:

dry ice ●
acid rain ■
poisonous hail ▲

T he coral reefs found around some
islands are formed of small animals
known as polyps and their:

food ●
habitat ■
skeletons ▲

C hameleons can change color to blend with their backgrounds. The plaice, a sea fish, can even match a checkerboard pattern. This technique is called:

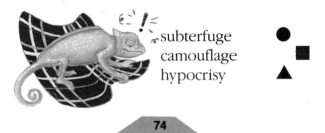

subterfuge ●

camouflage ■

hypocrisy ▲

T he hoatzin is a strange South American bird. Before knowing how to use its wings, it climbs trees thanks to what device found on its wings?

claws ●

suction cups ■

scales ▲

S talactites hang from the roofs of caves. They result from calcium deposits accumulated over thousands of years. Similar formations found on the ground of caves and that grow upwards are:

satellites ●
stalagmites ■
stigmata ▲

T o this day, some people still live in caves, whether in Turkey (Cappadocia) or the southwestern USA (Pueblo Indians). These people are called:

polyglots ●
globetrotters ■
troglodytes ▲

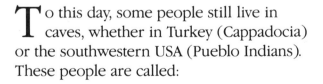

During the summer, cows are sent out of the barn and to mountain meadows to graze on the young grass. These grassy areas are known as:

tundra    
pastures
prairie

In order to sow seeds, the soil must first be tilled. When the seeds must be sown in rows, the soil must be plowed in:

furrows
bands
channels

S eeds in the ground absorb water. When roots appear, the plant is still feeding on its own seed. Once the roots are strong enough, the seed is exhausted. This is the end of:

ramification   
implantation
germination

M an creates artificial fields to give cattle necessary fodder. Once mown and dried, the hay is formed into:

haystacks
talus
wheat

Pruning consists of cutting a tree's old branches in order to let young ones grow correctly. One tool that's often used:

pruning shears ●
hammer ■
sprayer ▲

There exist cold regions where huge coniferous forests grow, and in which brown bears, moose, polar hares, etc., live. These regions are known as:

the desert ●
the savannah ■
the taiga ▲

M en used to fell trees with axes. Now they use power saws. These men are called:

loggers ●
foremen ■
farmers ▲

T he bocage is a landscape of fields and meadows. It is delineated by narrow bands of trees and shrubs known as:

beeches ●
hedges ■
underbrush ▲

S ummer is a short season in polar
regions. The cold weather keeps plants
from growing. During the winter, the sea is
covered by a thick layer of ice, called the:

skating rink ●
ice-pack ■
film ▲

T he equatorial forest includes hundreds
of different trees. They have huge
trunks and are always green. This forest is
also called:

the jungle ●
the equator ■
the tropic ▲

There are small islets of vegetation in the desert, where one finds water and fig trees, date trees, etc. These islets are called:

palm groves ●
paradise ■
oases ▲

In polar regions, huge blocks of ice sometimes go adrift. The submerged part accounts for ⅘ of their volume. These blocks of ice are called:

icebergs ●
icons ■
Inuits ▲

An atoll is usually a coral reef that forms a ring around a saltwater "lake." The "lake" is a(n):

islet • 

lagoon ■

peninsula ▲

Sand is made of tiny pieces of minerals torn from rocks by water and wind. The nature of the different minerals (quartz, clay) can explain the differences in sand's:

color •

shape ■

weight ▲

I n the mountains, low-altitude leafy forests give way to coniferous forests as altitude increases. Vegetation becomes even rarer higher up the mountains. The limit of growth is called the:

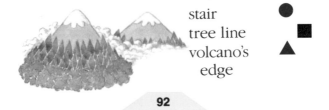

stair    ●
tree line    ■
volcano's    ▲
edge

T here are 7 continents on earth. Some countries, like Japan, Madagascar, an Greenland, are not attached to any continent, but are surrounded by water, which makes them:

deserts    ●
volcanoes    ■
islands    ▲

There are several types of still water. Among several names for such waters are ponds and:

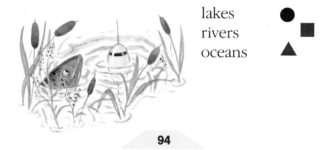

lakes
rivers
oceans

Nowadays, farmers are helped in their work by large machines. Thanks to combine harvesters, which harvest automatically, farmers no longer have to use manual tools such as:

windmills
sickles
millstones

S ome crops only grow in hot climates. This is particularly true of pineapples, cotton, coconuts, and:

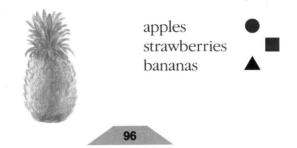

apples ●
strawberries ■
bananas ▲

S ome people's job is to observe nature. Specialists only study one subject in particular. Botanists only study plants, and ornithologists specialize in:

bees ●
birds ■
mammals ▲

The river empties into a lake, which, in turn, flows into another river, and then empties into the sea. The place where river and sea meet is called an estuary. The sides of all waterways are called shores or:

pediments
overflows
banks

Most bees live in apiaries that belong to apiculturists, who collect the honey. Wild bees live in tree trunks. These bee groups are called:

swarms
dens
wasps

Nature changes along with the seasons. Nature becomes dormant in autumn and reawakens in the spring. In the woods in spring snowdrops are the first new things to appear. They are:

flowers
trees
mushrooms

Ocean waves are due to the wind's effect on the water. The wave's height is due to the wind's intensity. Waves are always topped by a sort of froth known as:

dribble
foam
root

# Pollution

oil spills

waste

toxic gases

polluting products

factory waste

# Tree Leaves, Flowers and Fruits

pine

oak

beech

birch

chestnut

willow                    apple tree

cherry tree        maple

walnut

# Tree Bark

birch

chestnut

pine

willow

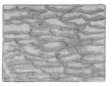

oak